THE NATIONAL POETRY SERIES

The National Poetry Series was established in 1978 to ensure the publication of five poetry books annually through participating publishers. Publication is funded by the Lannan Foundation; the late James A. Michener and Edward J. Piszek through the Copernicus Society of America; Stephen Graham; International Institute of Modern Letters; Joyce & Seward Johnson Foundation; Juliet Lea Hillman Simonds Foundation; and the Tiny Tiger Foundation. This project also is supported in part by an award from the National Endowment for the Arts, which believes that a great nation deserves great art.

NATIONAL
ENDOWMENT
FOR THE ARTS

D0191435

2005 COMPETITION WINNERS

Steve Gehrke of Columbia, Missouri,
Michelangelo's Seizure
Chosen by T. R. Hummer, University of Illinois
Press

Nadine Meyer of Columbia, Missouri,
The Anatomy Theater
Chosen by John Koethe, HarperCollins

Patricia Smith of Tarrytown, New York,
Teahouse of the Almighty
Chosen by Edward Sanders, Coffee House Press

S. A. Stepanek of West Chicago, Illinois,
Three, Breathing
Chosen by Mary Ruefle, Wave Books

Tryfon Tolides of Farmington, Connecticut,
An Almost Pure Empty Walking
Chosen by Mary Karr, Penguin Books

teahouse of the almighty

POEMS BY
Patricia Smith

COFFEE HOUSE PRESS
MINNEAPOLIS

Coffee House Press books are available to the trade through our primary distributor, Consortium Book Sales & Distribution, 1045 Westgate Drive, Saint Paul, MN 55114. For personal orders, catalogs, or other information, write to: Coffee House Press, 27 North Fourth Street, Suite 400, Minneapolis, MN 55401.

Coffee House Press is a nonprofit literary publishing house. Support from private foundations, corporate giving programs, government programs, and generous individuals help make the publication of our books possible. We gratefully acknowledge their support in detail in the back of this book.

Good books are brewing at coffeehousepress.org

LIBRARY OF CONGRESS
CATALOGING-IN-PUBLICATION DATA
Smith, Patricia
Teahouse of the almighty : poems / by Patricia Smith.
p. cm.
ISBN-13: 978-1-56689-193-6 (alk. paper)
ISBN-10: 1-56689-193-0 (alk. paper)
1. African Americans—Poetry. I. Title.
PS3569.M537839T43 2006
378.1'06—DC22
2006011899
FIRST EDITION | FIRST PRINTING
1 3 5 7 9 8 6 4 2
Printed in the United States

Grateful acknowledgment is made to the editors of the following publications where these poems first appeared: *Spirit and Flame: An Anthology of Contemporary African-American Poetry:* "Building Nicole's Mama," *Asheville Poetry Review:* "Map Rappin'," *Underwood Review:* "Forgotten in All This," *Willow Review:* "Teahouse of the Almighty," *Callaloo:* "Her Other Name."

Special thanks to Edward Sanders, and to the benefactors and supporters of the National Poetry Series; to Luis Rodriguez, Michael Warr, and Marc Smith for an invaluable birth; to Stephen Dobyns and Tom Lux for the friendship, support, and unflinching guidance; to the national poetry slam community and the staff and students of Cave Canem, and to Kwame Dawes, the perfect "go-to guy."

For Mikaila, The Face, who lights every corner of my world and work.

For Bruce, my doting husband and partner, the consummate editor.

For Damon, my son, who will prevail.

And for Boof! Fwa!

CONTENTS

If thou be more than hate or atmosphere
Step forth in splendor, mortify our wolves.
Or we assume a sovereignty ourselves.

—GWENDOLYN BROOKS

BUILDING NICOLE'S MAMA

for the 6th grade class of Lillie C. Evans School, Liberty City, Miami

I am astonished at their mouthful names—
Lakinishia, Fumilayo, Chevellanie, Delayo—
their ragged rebellions and lip-glossed pouts,
and all those pants drooped as drapery.
I rejoice when they kiss my face, whisper wet
and urgent in my ear, make me their obsession
because I have brought them poetry.

They shout me raw, bruise my wrists with pulling,
and brashly claim me as mama as they
cradle my head in their little laps,
waiting for new words to grow in my mouth.

You.
You.
You.
Angry, jubilant, weeping poets—we are all
saviors, reluctant hosannas in the limelight,
but you knew that, didn't you? Then let us
bless this sixth grade class—40 nappy heads,
40 cracking voices, and all of them
raise their hands when I ask. They have all seen
the Reaper, grim in his heavy robe,
pushing the button for the dead project elevator,
begging for a break at the corner pawn shop,
cackling wildly in the back pew of the Baptist church.

I ask the death question and forty fists
punch the air, *me!, me!* And O'Neal,
matchstick crack child, watched his mother's
body become a claw, and 9-year-old Tiko Jefferson,
barely big enough to lift the gun, fired a bullet
into his own throat after Mama bended his back
with a lead pipe. Tamika cried into a sofa pillow
when Daddy blasted Mama into the north wall
of their cluttered one-room apartment,
Donya's cousin gone in a drive-by. Dark window,
click, click, gone, says Donya, her tiny finger
a barrel, the thumb a hammer. I am shocked
by their losses—and yet when I read a poem
about my own hard-eyed teenager, Jeffery asks

He is dead yet?

It cannot be comprehended,
my 18-year-old still pushing and pulling
his own breath. And those 40 faces pity me,
knowing that I will soon be as they are,
numb to our bloodied histories,
favoring the Reaper with a thumbs-up and a wink,
hearing the question and shouting *me, me,*
Miss Smith, I know somebody dead!

Can poetry hurt us? they ask me before
snuggling inside my words to sleep.
I love you, Nicole says, Nicole wearing my face,
pimples peppering her nose, and she is as black
as angels are. Nicole's braids clipped, their ends

kissed with match flame to seal them,
and *can you teach me to write a poem about my mother?*
I mean, you write about your daddy and he dead,
can you teach me to remember my mama?

A teacher tells me this is the first time Nicole
has admitted that her mother is gone,
murdered by slim silver needles and a stranger
rifling through her blood, the virus pushing
her skeleton through for Nicole to see.
And now this child with rusty knees
and mismatched shoes sees poetry as her scream
and asks me for the words to build her mother again.
Replacing the voice.
Stitching on the lost flesh.

So poets,
as we pick up our pens,
as we flirt and sin and rejoice behind microphones—
remember Nicole.
She knows that we are here now,
and she is an empty vessel waiting to be filled.

And she is waiting.
And she
is
waiting.
And she waits.

GIVING BIRTH TO SOLDIERS

February 1, 2005—Tabitha Bonilla's husband, Army Captain Orlando A. Bonilla, 27, was killed Wednesday in a helicopter accident in Baghdad. Her father, Army Sergeant First Class Henry A. Bacon, 45, died in Iraq last February.

She will pin ponderous medals to her
housedress, dripping the repeated roses,
while she claws through boxes filled with
him and then him. The accepting of God's
weird wisdom takes place over forkfuls
of rubbery casseroles and the snowy vows
of newsmen who measure her worth
in cued weeping. She offers her husband's
hands, a shrine of their mingled smells,
a warm seat on a couch of napped corduroy.
They offer one polished bone, scrubbed
clean of war. And she babbles of links and
irony, shrugs her numb shoulders, and feels
dimly blessed as a door slams shut on both
sides of her head. Suddenly, she is her
only history. Smiling politely beneath a fierce
salute, propped upright behind the crumpled
ghosts of her men, she is the catchy logo
for a confounded country. This day is the day
she has. Tomorrow, she will touch her own
breasts, she will dismantle a gaudy altar
with her teeth. And she will ask a bemused God
for guidance as she steps back into line,
her womb tingling vaguely with the next soldier.

IT HAD THE BEAT INEVITABLE

It's all right what Bobby Womack taught us, what Chaka growled,
o.k. to flaunt the hard stone double dutch planted in our calves.

Forgive Smokey for sending us off to search for that white horse
and the half-white boy riding it. Go on, shove that peppermint stick

down the center of that sour pickle, dine on a sandwich of Wonder
and souse, take your stand in that black woman assembly line to

scrape the scream from chitlins. It's all right that Mama caught the
'hound up from Alabama, that Daddy rode up from Arkansas and

you're the only souvenir they got. We brown girls, first generation
brick, sparkling in Dacron and pink sweat socks, we went the only

way we could. Our weather vane, whirling in Chicago wind, was the
rusted iron torso of a stout black woman. We vanished for a while.

Gwen Brooks hissed *Follow*. We had no choice.

MISSISSIPPI'S LEGS

for Koko Taylor

It was black out there.
The starless Alabama night
pressed against my skin,
hard like a man, steam I couldn't fathom.
I was 14. I was trouble.
My chest bulged with wrong moving
and other women's men lapped up my smell—
the smell of a gun barrel
once the bullet is gone.
Fat flies, blood loony and irritated by the moon,
nibbled at my ankles and buzzed *sweet Jesus*
when they tasted the thick sweet oil
I rubbed in to make my legs shine.
I was 14. My hips were wide, keening.
I had lightning bolts for legs.

Wrinkled women, grateful for the sleeping sun,
shucked peas, ripped silk from corn,
rocked do-diddy rhythms on fallen porches.
Boys with earth naps screeched crave into the air
and waited for answers and somewhere
a man named *J.T.* or *Diamond* or *Catfish*
blew everything he had into a harp
and hollered when he found his heart,
still moist and pumping,
lying at the bottom of a shot glass.

Everybody wanted a way up and out of that town,
a town so small, such a fist of heat and no stars,
that I was able to tuck it all into my cheek
before I stood on my long brown lightning legs
and flew.

The backhand slap that stopped me was called Chicago.
I ran into the first open door
and screamed Mississippi into a microphone,
knocking out most of my teeth in the process.
The men, long cool wisps of glimmer,
fed me whiskey, dressed me red, called me *baby,*
laid me down in their king beds,
mapped my widening body, flowered me.
At night I swallowed their cigarette smoke,
swiveled my fat, and gave them Mississippi—
the proper name for the growing larger,
the blue black, the heavy ankles,
the stiff store-bought auburn flip. By then,
I had to be dead to leave.

Now I sit and watch the white girls
wiggle in to ask for my signing on something.
They wait till they think my back is turned
and they laugh at the black hole of my mouth,
the spilling out, my red wig sweat-sliding.
They wonder how I stuff all this living
into lamé two sizes too gold,
laugh at how I write my name real slow.
I just tap my slingback, smile real grateful-like,
wait till they try to leave. Then I grab one of 'em,

haul her back by that stringy perfumed head,
and growl what the city taught me:

You hearin' me? You hear?

I might not have but one tooth left.
But at least

it's gold.

walloping! magnifying of a guy's anatomy easily

Subject line for a junk e-mail touting a "penile enhancer"

Emmett was all pelvis, theatrics
in lieu of heft and measure.
I threw Rich out of bed
and made him dance naked
in the hall. His spurt was ludicrous.
A.J.'s cocked to the left,
dots of Hai Karate flowering
his testes. And the bubbled one
with gut smothering the stub.
Florid dramas of the teeny weenie,
the entertainments of strut,
snug synthetic fibers, blustery spiels.
And now this little yellow pill
that grows even history huge.
And easily. Yes, and damn.

1.

Begin with the rhythm of chapped hands traversing
the naked hips of a Raelette. Begin with the whispered
boundaries of a gone world. Forced to craft other English,
men stutter with their surfaces, jump when they touch
something raw. At birth, the cottony light of the real grew
faint until music swelled its arcing arms and claimed him.
At the very second of heaven, a history swerved close,
teased, but did not return. He said good-bye to strangers.

2.

What heaven would have him, ashed, so much of hollow,
now irritably whole? Imagine the gasping and gulping, the
sputtered queries at the sight of sunflowers and foil. There's
a holy niche in hell for these harbingers of hard wisdoms,
men with this strain of jazz in them, men who have seen the
inward of women, heard colors settle, eased shameful things
into their mouths. The Last Rapture is best without his kind,
without his crazed seeing knock splintering the gilded wood.

3.

Which is the kill that repeats: To lose what you have seen, or
never to see what you have already lost? And the ears become
earth drums, huge hands, vessels. They rush to scream him
everything, including dust, cerulean, the moist blinking of a
woman's hip. Even touch gets loud, shocking his long fingers,

jolting him upright in the damnable dark. His days become
his skin, blank and patient. Even when bellowed, many words,
like *today* and *never,* translate to nothing truly seen or known.

4.

Sudden mothers, lying clocks, warm canes. Women are
everywhere. He has buckled beneath their gazing, knowing
how truly they see him, straining erect, eyes bop-do-ditty in
a bobbing head. He allows them their pity strolls across his
map while he moves his palms up and down, flat against their
waiting faces, reading, reading. They stink so good, and he is
amazed at their talent for tangling the recalled. But they talk
too damned much. All those split declaratives deny his eyes.

5.

The politics of smooth and unpuckered, the sounds of a man
reciting what he will never know. What separates the living of
this from the dying of it, it is all that no-color, that hugest of
sound, the din, fingertips swollen from touching everything
twice, the dim wattage of time crawling beyond where it was.
Faces, angle and ghost, rise up to him, dance their mean
little circumstance dance, claim the simplest drifting names.
Slamming all his eyes against them only carves the hard loss.

6.

Promise drips from songs, but the heart can't see anything.

7.

The body, snide prankster, won't stop. Tumbling through sheets
leaves a bright sting. The right music ignites even the flattest ass.
Damned toes tap. Anything on the tongue must be swallowed or

expelled. The gut fills, piss trickles. Eyes flap open, even though.
The elbow cranks, the cock stiffens, roots of thirst and addictions
thicken. The sun bakes blank recollection on open skin. Inside him
a wretched world spins, machine unerring, striving for such a silly
perfect. The body doesn't need moonwash or windows. It just churns.

8.

His pulse has the gall to beat urgently, like it does when one spies
a familiar canvas or a lostago sweet. It's as if one of his strangers
has dangled life's pointed, two-pronged instruction just inside the
void: *Remember what you have seen. See what you remember.* He
spends his days straining toward either or both of these squiggling
concepts, building whole novels on a hint of ginger riding someone's
breath. In the end, almost buried by his sad collage, he clings to a
single truth: Whenever he asks for water, it arrives. It always arrives.

9.

When a gone man dies, what could possibly be taken away? It must
be the light that leaves, darkening even places it has never touched.

10.

Salvation blesses him with gasping eyes, pinned open and glaring,
and hours that slide like silver over his skin. The first thing he sees
is everything. His whole life hurtles past, paining him with its
scarlets and excess, the pulsing soundtrack a sweet irritant. The
first thing he sees is all of it, the interminable meetings, the mercy
fucks, a sweaty tumbler of ice water, finally his own knees. Eternity
is this looped, unblinking cinema of himself. Paradise is crammed
with the cruelly blessed struck dumb by scenes too loud to live.

THE WORLD WON'T WAIT

On Tuesday, I watched as a 27-year-old man
held an electric toothbrush in his hand.
His fingers fumbled a bit at the switch,
but he flipped it, then sat astounded
as the dry brush shimmied and jumped in his palm.

This run on batteries?, he asked,
turning it upside down,
his eyes lit with a toddler's wonder.

Perhaps you see nothing amazing in this.
But let me paint a picture of this man.

His chest is impossibly plumped, thick and rigid,
his skin mapped with stretch marks
where the muscle has exploded beneath.
His shaved head, a field of grizzle and sweet spray,
is peppered with gouges where the blade sensed
his blood and slipped. He is a child of single syllables,
grunts just under the radar:
I need to eat.
I'm real tired.
Think it's gon' rain.
I like that shirt.
He is my

son, crafted of fevers unleashed and jailhouse iron.
And now, with the clear beyond cry, I see
that his punishment was never there,
among the scabbed tattoos, sluggish clocks, open toilets.
His sentence began in the free, in that moment
when he turned a cheap chugging red toothbrush
over and over in his huge hands and said,
Look at this, Ma. Wow, look at this.

LISTENING AT THE DOOR

Beneath the door, I could practically see
the wretched slither of tobacco and English Leather.
Hiding on the other side, I heard Mama giggle
through clenched teeth, which meant potential
husband sitting spitshined on our corduroy couch.
The needle hit that first groove and I wondered
why my mama had chosen the blues,
wrong, Friday-angled, when it was hope
she needed. I pressed my ear against the door,
heard dual damp panting, the Murphy bed squeal,
the occasional directive,
the sexless clink of jelly jar glasses.

What drove me to listen on those nights
when my mother let that fragrant man in,
banished me to the back of the apartment,
pretended she could shine above hurting?
I'd rest my ear against the cool wood all night
as she flipped through the 45s—
looking for Ray Charles, Stevie Wonder,
somebody blind this time,
somebody crawling on his knees toward love.

THE END OF A MARRIAGE

is totally silent, eerie in its zero.
Not even the clunk of paralleled possessions
dropping into cardboard boxes or the satisfying
slamming of doors, one after another, can slap
a period on chaos. It's just one syrupy moon-eyed
gaze, taking in his overlapped belly, the dangerous
mole dotting her left shoulder, the blue veins
like roads to death behind his knees. It's that watery
stare with no stop, the frenzied gulping of line,
curve, voice, all the stark unbended was of them.

Yes, we flinched against the losing, even our venom
was distinctly hued. Everyone kept asking, begging
detail, but all there was was the utter nothing, just
our eyes locked on our eyes, traversing that ragged
territory once more for the record, finally dropping
abruptly from the edge of my body, the edge of his.
It was a threadbare connect meant to end tragically,
one that was broken when we blinked and he turned
away and I turned away, our eyes fused open.
Then we began our walk toward separate sounds.

BOY DIES, GIRLFRIEND GETS HIS HEART

Patterson, Calif. (AP)—A 15-year-old boy who learned that his girlfriend needed a heart transplant told his mother three weeks ago that he was going to die and that the girl should have his heart. Felipe Garza, who his brother said had seemed in perfect health, died Saturday after a blood vessel burst in his head. His family followed his wishes, and Felipe's heart was transplanted Sunday into Donna Ashlock.

The deep things we know.
How systems grow restless
and damning in us,
stunning the machine.
And what we feel.
The head romances us,
coos anxious wooings,
makes us want to lie back
and listen to the failures,
the bones thinning,
fat clogging the paths.
Outside us, what?
Some opening waiting to scar over.
Some flower peeled open,
its drum growing slow.
And, suddenly, the least we can do is us.

Patterson, Calif. (AP)—A 17-year-old girl, who three years ago received the heart of a boyfriend who died, needs a new heart because her body is rejecting the transplanted organ. Doctors are looking for a suitable heart for Donna Ashlock, who has been living with the heart of Felipe Garza since Jan. 4, 1986. Doctors learned last month that the Garza heart has been permanently damaged by Donna's body's repeated attempts to reject it.

I want this earth out of me,
this conjured world, this wire,
this battery, this button.
I would rather the suddening stoplight,
the dawned silence.
Beat it backwards, shoot it through
with slivers of glass, chop it from its walls.
Arise it beyond me, make it arc
over my dead head like a heaven.
Imagine the given thing being all you are.
Imagine a machine's steel tear.
Know how I know this cannot be my heart.
It loves me too much.

Patterson, Calif. (AP)—Donna Ashlock, the 17-year-old girl whose body rejected the transplanted heart of a boyfriend, died Tuesday while waiting for a new heart.

Heaven is a room without air,
tinier than you would expect.
Their harbors summarily discarded,
souls are smashed upon souls,
writhing, lit neon with overwhelms of holy.
Here names, crimes, and choices
are forgotten. There is only one door,
and the harried souls hurtle through,
bargain for space, pulse gleefully.
The fickle, traitorous heart is a need
no one misses. In heaven,
they keep one beating
in a cage, purely for show.

DUMPSTERS, WASTEBASKETS, SHALLOW GRAVES

I almost learned this in my almost life: Breathe
like your living depends on it. Here is something
I almost remember—Mama's prickly translation
of hold, belief strained. In the first hopeful instant
she held me, slip slide in looped chenille, scarlet
coil marring my belly, wee head sweatstuck to the
crook of her arm, my tiny chest had rockets inside.
One finger moved my wet, slick hair into pattern,
traced the shadow of my slowing heart. I learned
that swallowing once will not feed you. I learned
the brief language of a poking finger. And because
I cried so little and learned so well, she imagined
a misting future. She almost gave me a name.

TO 3, NO ONE IN THE PLACE

Ignore the crack in rhythm, the mangled lyrics,
my face stunned under sticky layers of cinnamon
and rose. I drew the woman you wanted. I spritzed
Chanel in my throat shadows and in a line inside
my thighs to my knees. I shaved landscapes,
shunned underwear, colored my nails bitterly red.
And then, just ten minutes to show,
I studied my angles of craving.
I will hoist myself up onto the ancient Steinway,
drag a blue feather boa along the gleam, tilt my head,
and separate the limelight into merely a million angels.

When I was 16, my hips moved like they had water in them.
When I was 22, men in patent clickers and sharkskin suits
couldn't say my name without weeping. I sang them to sleep,
then left. By 30, I had set fire to the names of two husbands.
Everything I crooned was pissed and indigo. Now I'm warbling
beneath a shifting layer of 40, bound to a sad stash of ballads
anyone with a steady tongue and half a dream could sing.

There's my half a dream over there, barely recognizable
as you, slumped in your seat at a quarter to leaving,
not knowing or caring if I ever got around to that song
you asked for with a wink, a single sweaty dollar.
You wanted to hear "My Romance," which I sang
like any more breathing I planned to do depended on it.
I cooed, flirted, and crawled my whole self into every note,
and when I came up for air, I knew you hadn't heard it.

I was backdrop, I was time passing, I was hey somebody
get me one more whiskey, I was did the rain start yet,
I was bet those tits aren't real, I was wish she was younger,
I was at least the piano player's decent, I was damned
drinks are watered down, I was I can't believe I blew
this much cash, I was bet she was hot 20 years ago,
I was where's the john?, I was damn she blew *that* note,
I was should I wait around?, I was fuck, it's all the same
in the dark, I was hope this old piece a' ass is worth it,
I was is she ever gonna stop singing?, I was oh yeah
feelin' that Chivas, I was did she ever sing that song,
whatever the hell it was, that sappy shit I paid her to sing?

There's a back door to this place. I use it sometimes.
But first I have to face the dressing room's endless mirrors,
where the wronged songstress sees herself repeated,
where I scrub off four layers of sweetened skin,
ease folded toes out of tortuous pumps, and pray away
the broad ache in my throat. There's a tap on the door
and I think maybe it's the manager with my cash
or this week's excuse for not having my cash. But it's you,
rumpled and bleary, dangerous because you've peeked
my dreaming, because you are the lie I've decided to hear.
You want the whole heart of the millionth angel.
Cue the woo of surrender, the sloppy fuck with soundtrack.

SACRIFICE

*"Twenty eight Chilean women stripped naked in the middle of a busy
road in Santiago, Chile, to pay homage to poet Pablo Neruda..."*
—UPI, 1/2/2005

"Naked you are simple as one of your hands"
—"Morning: Love Sonnet XXVII," Neruda

Flustered, without license or sanction, the women
clawed at whispered cotton and lopsided seam,
pushed irritants to their ankles, and stood upright
for whole seconds, just long enough for nipples
to pimple in soft wind. Behind them, a home that
once held his pens, his grimace acknowledging
a tumbled phrase, earthquakes that grew pliant
in him, and now twenty-eight quick asses framed
in the window. Much too rushed for structure, the
photographer did what he could to stun the slow
chaos—heads were twisted, eyes in blink, pubic
hair indistinct and shadowed. As sirens wailed,
the women hurried into their clothes—blouses
with nervy stink circles, skirts accordioned in haste.
Their names were nothing and they were rootless
in their wandering away. There was no sense
to their sacrifice, until the night came and the poet's
slow remembering hands returned for their souls.

MY MILLION FATHERS, STILL HERE PAST

Hallelujah for grizzled lip, snuff chew, bended slow walk,
and shit talkin'. Praise fatback, pork gravy, orange butter,
Alaga syrup, grits, and egg sammiches on Wonder Bread
slathered with Hellman's, mashed 'tween sheets of wax
paper. You hoard that food like money. You are three-day
checker games, pomade slick back, deep brown drink
sucked through holes where teeth once was. You're that
can't-shake lyric, that last bar stool before the back door.

All glory to the church deacons, bodies afloat in pressed
serge, nappy knobs of gray hair greased flat, close to conk,
cracked tenors teetering and testifying. Bless you postmen
and whip cloth shoeshiners, foremen with burning backs,
porters bowing deep. I hear swear-scowling and gold-tooth
giggling over games of bid whist and craps, then Sunday's
Lucky Struck voices playing call-and-response with
the Good Book's siren song. In the midst of some hymn,
my wilting fathers, I see you young again, you spitshined
and polished, folded at the hips on a sluggish Greyhound,
or colored in the colored car of a silver train chugging past
Pine Bluff, Aliceville, Minneola, Greenwood, Muscle Shoals,
headed north where factories pumped precise gospel
and begged you inside their open mouths. You're the reason

the Saturday moon wouldn't fall. You mail-order zoot suit
wide wing felt hats to dip low over one eye, pimp walkin',
taps hammered into heels, kickin' up hot foot to get down

one time, slow drag blues threading bone and hip bump
when the jukebox teases. All praise to the eagle what flew
on Friday and the Lincoln Mark, the Riviera, the Deuce
and a Quarter, the always too much car for what you were.
You were lucky number, the dream book, the steaming spoon
of black-eyes on day one of every year. Here is to your mojo,
your magic real, roots and conjures and long-dead plants
in cotton pouches. Deftly misled by tiny religions, you spat
on the broom that brushed your foot, stayed left of light poles.

Griots of sloped porch and city walk, you, my million fathers,
still here past chalk outlines, dirty needles, and prison cots,
still here past ass whuppings, tree hangings, and many calls
to war, past J.B. stupor, absent children, and drive-bys.
You survive, scarred and hobbling, choking back dawn ache,
high pressure, dimming and lying eyes, joints that smell thunder.
Here's to the secret of your rotting molars, the tender bump
on your balls, your misaligned back, wild corn on that baby
toe, the many rebellions of your black, tired bodies. I watch
you cluck the hard history of lust past your gums, squeeze
rheumy eyes shut to conjure the dream outline of a woman.

I am a woman.
I will rub your weary head,
dance close to you,
shuck you silver peas for dinner.

He was Otis, my father.
But you are Willie Earl and James and Ernest and Jimmy Lee.
All of you, frail charmers, gentle Delta, bodies curled against
the time gone, the time coming. I grieve you tottering toward

death, I celebrate you clinging to life. Open bony dark-veined
arms and receive me, a woman in the shape of your daughter,
who is taking on your last days as her very blood, learning
your whispered language too late to stop your dying,
but not too late
to tell
this story.

HOW TO BE A LECHEROUS LITTLE OLD BLACK MAN AND MAKE LOTS OF MONEY

for John Lee Hooker

First, you got to get the blues.
This is easy if you are a person of any gender,
and possess a pulse, a cheating lover,
a stalking ex-lover, a used Yugo, a pumping heart,
an empty wallet, a half-dead dog, an empty frigerator,
one last cigarette butt, a good memory, a nosy mama,
a lonely room, a quick trigger, roving eyes,
an addiction to whiskey,
nothing but the clothes on your back,
a jones for your neighbor's wife,
a jones for your wife's neighbor,
a positive test result,
an itching to leave,
an itching to stay,
or any itching where there shouldn't be any.

Rub your hands slow over your body,
feel the valleys, the wrongs. Let misery
chomp your spine toward collapsing,
let it fold your whole self double.
Then you can walk like John Lee Hooker do—
click shuffle, bent over, nose to the ground,
wearing a cocked brim felt fedora that wouldn't dare fall off.
Then you can think like John Lee do—
I'm old as victrola,

gotta buy a bottle of Mrs. Butterworth
if I want to feel a woman,
but I can still

sing better

than you

HALLELUJAH WITH YOUR NAME

I.

Perhaps I underestimate his importance.
After all, he was merely a crooked arm, a suit coat
dripping pressed shine, Old Spice and Wild Turkey
lending his soul a smell. He was just a flattened
and knowing hand at the small of my back, he was
nothing more than bended knees trying to match
his height to mine. The bartop was slick and glittering
with something, one leg of the jukebox propped up
too high on a cardboard square. Ask why
I remember that he never bothered to take off his
storm gray Stetson, that a single sweet thread
of sweat ran down the left side of his face, kissing
our clasped hands. I was 1 2, clacking knees, high-top
All Stars with flap tongues, a wad of grape bubble
plumping my cheek. He was a friend of my father's,
his name wavering now between Willie and Earl.
He was grizzled and elegant, horrifying man-smell,
bowing slightly for permission to lead the woman
in me across a slice of pockmarked wooden floor.
Daddy grinned and hooted in the face of this crime.

II.

Slow dancing is the way sin looks when you hose
it down and set it upright, and all the time it is
the considering of further things, the music being
incidental, it might as well not be there. You can slow

dance to a dollop of chocolate, a wrinkled shred of silk,
the hot static of a child's hair being brushed. Drag slow
on top of an angry lover's silence, along the jittery
borders of a rain ring, on the cluttered sidewalk outside
wherever you are. You can dance to the arcing brows
of folks wondering why you have stopped to dance. Under
the thinnest pretense, you can demand touch. Without
considering consequence, you can sign your body over.

III.

By the time of that first slow dance, I had tasted
stormwater, head cheese, starch, sweet pickle juice.
In raw sanctified churches, I was swathed in crinoline
and dipped, hair first, into whatever wouldn't kill me.
I knew how to fight for my life with a bottleneck.
I had discovered the liquid verb of my hips and had
gnawed the vinegary meat from the foot of a pig.
I could slip a thousand coins through the slot
of a juke, knowing my backbone would respond to
any song, any old keyed wail from a shattered someone.
I could exist on unclean things, slippery with fat,
and crush hugely pregnant roaches with the heel
of my hand. I dared slow-sputter four-syllable words.
Daddy taught me to be constantly astonishing.

IV.

The man who taught me to slow dance was simply
my father's friend, who lifted me from a wobbling
stool when I nodded yes. He was that first gracious
sweep, flat laboring feet, slapped smile, awkward
realizing that a memory was coming to life in his arms.

The song? A woman was moaning so hard the record
skipped to save her. She was leaving, thinking
of leaving or had left, or someone had left her.
She had nothing left. My partner off-key spittled
every third word, flashing a gold incisor that made
me move closer to him. I wanted to get all of him
over with, to squeeze his scarecrow body through
and past me. I wanted us history. I knew then why
it is always the woman who dances backwards,
numbing her short spine, circling the man's neck
with both arms. She is scrambling for a glimpse
of where she's been, the yesterday she had before
he gets hard and confuses hallelujah with her name.

LITTLE POETRY

He says I am gumpopper,
   wondrous shoulders,
evil on the days when I bleed.

I say take hold of both my hands.
   He speaks cool water on me,
nudges my mood with a proverb.

I watch him undress, skin
   unto another skin, and I turn
away to keep from craving that.

By the time his hands
   touch my shoulders,
I am almost insane

with disappearing,
and the thunder.

CAN'T HEAR NOTHING
FOR THAT DAMNED TRAIN

Chaos, all sound and stench, everywhere the delirium
of the ordinary. Mamie Tuttle holds court on a lopsided
wooden porch, clearly an afterthought to her house, yelping
so sideways her gold tooth rattles: *Got room in my chair*
if anybody need it, scratching scalp, pressing hair, $5,
make you look good this Sunday!—all of her rollicking,
her greasy hands on world hips. For a hot minute, her spiel
drowns out the Temptations moaning for crazy love from
beneath a good girl's window. Lanky boys in worn-through
sharkskin snag the harmony, croon its bottom while Mamie,
diseased ankles damned tired now, declares *O.K. dammit, $4!*
Her answer is the cringe roll of cars on last rim, the squealed
lyric of double dutch girls pumping some God outta their legs.

Despite the sugar noise and veiled shit, you would think we'd
want out. The dying engineered green of Garfield Park, a planned
paradise of rust and splinter, is crushed into its corner, wailing
toward the world and Mamie, who is about to nap and could give
a damn: There's someplace better,
someplace lusher,
someplace past any reach you can reach.

Cover your ears.
Here comes the train.
That's where it's going.

DRINK, YOU MOTHERFUCKERS

"Tequila is a pallid flame that passes through walls and soars over tile roofs to allay despair."
   —*Alvaro Mutis*

Sergio was for no shit
that night. He was serving
up the blade juice, heavy-handed,

the sugary gold
sloshing over the tops
of much-thumbed tumblers.
Story was he rinsed
his glasses in gin to make sure
the germs were dead.

Well, no matter. That night
he was pinpoint focused
on laying his regulars flat

with fountains of Cuervo,
free for the time being
because he said it was.

The open mic,
an odd parade of eggshells
and desperadoes, had limped

to its usual anticlimax,
each poet duly convinced
that his lines had leapt

from the cocktail napkin,
sliced through the din,
and changed Chicago.

Now, no more
of those bare offerings,
florid lyrics of tomorrow and gray.

The doors were locked.
The M.C. was atilt, souvenir bras
dripped from the ceiling

and the johns smelled like snow.
This was world enough,
a timed blathering of our sad biographies,

Playtex as décor,
and an overwrought
of fever water spewing

from the grimy hands
of an insane Mexican barkeep.

When we slowed,
choking on the bitter kick
as he poured and poured,

Serge bellowed a thick-tongued
threat: *This ain't no joke. Drink,
you motherfuckers.*

He waved a sudden gun,
a clunky thing that sparked
snickers until he blasted

a hole in the ceiling and
revised our endings,
smalling our big drunken lives.

DELTATEACH
for all my mamas

delta teach me the sound
my heart makes when it
bends over backwards
to curse at its beat delta got
church stuffed in size 16,
carrying my gottahave milk,
telling me that i can make my

ownself feel good   just
when i'm thinking it might
take a man to make me feel
natural

delta teach me fatback,
skillet bread, hogshead,
alaga, drive me crazy with
warm grease, fatten me up
so that i can find
my second mouth

when my living be broken
delta help me find the piece
that can still shout the little bit
that can still squeeze into
a shiny thing and go downtown
where you can

sing about it, girl, sing about it,
pray hard over it, lean into it,
work with it, fry that thang up,
flip it, cut it loose, set fire
to it, turn it over, turn it out,
make it beg, go down on it,
call it sugar out loud, get wide
for it, lie to it, lie for it, lie
with it, but baby, don't let it kill you.

delta let me rub her throat
while she sing she
three-weave her fingers
while she sing she
wiggle like revelation
while she sing she
peel back my grinning
show everybody that lie
she find underneath there
she rip out the hooks
that man done left in my skin
ignores my pained wailing
bleeds   me

delta sponge me down with
pan water dab cheap smellgood
on my shattered shoulders
call me sista when she have to
baby when she want to
and fool most of the time

delta drive her mouth all over me
feeds me pure butter from a
teaspoon make me come like i
never have then she sing me some
aspirin she sing me edged hooch. she
ignores all those eyes. she take me
so dancing

CREATIVELY LOVED

for Raymond Wood Jr., 1994–1995

I was a foot tall, charming, tot stupid,
bump stumbling, a rumble lump of less
than future. It took me minutes to die,
my self blurring and curled like a comma
in leaving, Newport stubs damp candles
in my hair. Rayie Wood Jr., pesky shard
in the hip of the world. Why else would
you lift me above your head, slam me
to tile, lift me up again by my legs, swing
me against the closed door wicked enough
to splinter Wood, call me sugary names,
oh so sweet bastard me? But I thank you

father for the patient teaching of screech,
for drenching my one tooth in blood.
Thank you daddyman, for the alphabet
of the floorboards, thank you mother
for the live matches against me. Thank
you *SHUT* father for the ripe *THE FUCK
UP* loving in your mouth, thank you for
YOU LITTLE the slam and the smash me
BASTARD and for the bounce and the
rattle, for the drama of cut beginning.

How else would I learn the huge love in
red hiss kisses, the shining purpose of me?

ELEGANTLY ENDING
for Ella Fitzgerald

A lyric unravels,
spins on dizzied axis,
one syllable slinks
and becomes several.

A stark shaft of light
illuminates a never-over evolution.
Each exhalation
excites and concludes

with a slight upturn
of phrase that compromises
the hip, roots fat legs,
lends such southern heave to torso.

Mysteries thrive in the belly
and in the miraculous
of her throating,
send two errant verbs

round 'bout themselves
and into the keys
of her spine again.
It is not for us to know

her trilling suddenly
murderous and cringe
beautiful, inbound.
Her legs gone.

A lack of this elegance
is the end of evolution.
Consider the soundless hole.
Over.

SEX AND MUSIC

Imagine my disgust at discovering that I am
actually that readable and uncomplicated,
that I could find nothing in me worth noting
except one heat and two ways to release it.
Music leads to sex leads to music leads to sex.
If it wasn't for the clock of music imitating
the pulse of sexing someone, I could forego
this lapdance in my own lap. There's no need
for that sliver of ice, those chilly silver utensils,
the banshee howl, that two-way mirror,
the pliable circle of the mouth, Todd Rundgren's
Healing, that spread-eagle, the lazy drip of any
liquid, the ritual reading of Sharon Olds, that
imprint of your urgent ass marring my wall.

I can blame you on all this, your drumbeat hip,
what writhes in your pants. I can't stop sparking
what I keep having to douse. Kiss me that deep.
Turn the air into victim with your arms.
Dance me till weeping and the beauteous burn.

MAP RAPPIN'

for John Coltrane, and forever for Bruce

I always shudder when I pray.

Mama say the Lord enters you in stages,
first like a match lit under your skin,
then like an animal biting through bone
with soft teeth. Mama say lie still
and wait for glory to consume you,
wrap its way into your map
like a lover had his finger on paradise,
knew the way with all his heart, then lost it.
I always shudder when I pray,
so your name must be a prayer.
Saying your name colors my mouth,
frees loose this river, changes my skin,
turns my spine to string. I pray all the time now.
Amen.

Try not to touch me while I tell this.
Try not to brush the thick tips of your fingers
against my throat while my throat moves
telling this story. Don't suddenly squeeze
my bare shoulder or travel your mouth
along the flat swell of my belly.
Don't bite at the hollow in my back,
whisper touch my ankles,
or match our skin like spoons.

Don't punctuate this rambling sentence
with your tongue or trace your name
on the backs of my legs,
please don't walk the question
of your breath along my thighs
or draw a map on my quivering breastbone
guiding me to you,
me to you,
me to you,
don't play me
that way

don't play me

that way

the way the saxman plays his woman,
blowing into her mouth till she cries,
allowing her no breath of her own.
Don't play me that way, baby, the way
the saxman plays his lady,
that strangling, soft murder—notes like bullets,
riffs like knives and the downbeat slapping
into her. and she sighs.
into her. and she cries.
into her.
and she whines like the night turning.

Let me sit here on the bar stool sipping something bitter.
Let me cross my legs,
slow

like the colored girls do,
and let me feel your eyes go there.
Let me feed on glory and grow fat.

Meanwhile, lover, let's fill this wicked church with music.
Let me lean into this story, for once,
without your mouth on me. The music a lit match
under my skin and I dance,
all legs and thunderous and heels too high,
I dance cheap perfume and black nail polish.
Sharkskin congregation, heads *pressed,*
attitudes too tight, won't scream
until it gets to be too much, won't beg for mercy
until I wreck the landscape with my hips.
Bar stools filling, everybody waiting for the glory
to move through me, fill me with hosannas,
rock me with hallelujahs, to shake these bored bones.
They wait for you, supreme love, to pull me out
onto the dance floor, make me kick my heels above my head.
High heels 'bove my nappy head.

While they wait, I will dance with the saxman,
I will shimmer as he presses my keys.
Him and me boppin', we are *wicked* church.
So don't play, do not play, did you hear me tell you
not to play me that way?
(The way I pray to be played.)

Mama say the Lord enters you in stages
(Play me that way)
First like a lit match under your skin

(Play me that way)
Then like an animal biting through bone with soft teeth
(Play me)
Mama say lie still and wait for glory
(that way)
to consume me
(that way)
Press my keys
(that way)
Press my keys
(that way)

Don't pay me no mind, lover.
I always shudder

when I pray.

IN THE AUDIENCE TONIGHT

for Philip

She is unnerved, anxious
at the state of the world,
but he insists that she uncoil.
The fluorescent light overhead
leaves her stretched bare,
vaguely ashamed of the ease
with which she's been translated.

In her language, exclamations
are held in the mouth
until they are too weak to escape.
They are both the children
of their absent fathers. His dad
was a sleek guitar neck,
hers a gritty dollop of Delta
cocky behind the steering of a car
propped up on northern wheels.

Their fathers are the dead
puppeteers who push them
toward one another
then pull them apart,
who jerk tangled strings
and teach them the blues out loud.
It will be hard to recall a time
when they were exactly

what they are now,
poised to become all of it
in spite of themselves.
His singing burns
like the blue sun
inked on his forearm.
She fully intends one word
to turn the earth's heart.

Such merriment
as the fathers watch their children.
They're those cackling, unruly ghosts
taking up no space at all in the third row,
the ones who tipped in
when the room's back was turned.
Guffawing until Camel spittle
and penny whiskey
spew from their grins,
they bob bony noggins
to the blue grind
and sing along.
They love that their offspring
waste their time so valiantly,
shapeshifting,
offering their verse and voltage
to crowds of solemn drunks,
hanging for all they're worth
to one cracking point of a star.

WEAPON ULTIMATE

The Nigerian women smeared
a thick line of Texaco's oil
under each eye, warrior warnings,
then crouched low and sprang
with the boulders of their bodies,
their stout ashy legs and mad wrists,
holding their paper banners with words
scratched out and respelled:
Give work to our husbands,
our brothers, our sons.
Give us light and water,
or pack now.
The pure singular force
of themselves.
Their glorious damnable throats.
You remember. Pack now.
Remember.

SCRIBE

My son, budding dreadhead, has taken a break from obsessively twisting and waxing his naps, swelling his delts, and busting rhymes with no aim, backbeat, or future beyond the common room. For want of a plumper canteen, the child has laid claim to a jailhouse vocation.

I'm the writer, Mama, he tells me.
That's what I'm known for in here.

In my kitchen, clutching the receiver, I want to laugh, because my son has *always* been the writer, muttering witness to the underbelly, his rebel heart overthumping, his bladed lines peppered with ready-market gangster swerve and cringing in awe of themselves. I want to laugh, but

I must commit to my focus. I must be typical, single, black, with an 18-to-30-year-old male child behind bars. How deftly I have learned the up/back of that tiring Watusi.

I guess it's a poem, he'd mutter.
Throw it away if you want.

And oh, I'd ache at what he'd done, the bottoms he'd found, the clutch he claimed on what refused to be held, the queries scraped from surface. *What are you chile?,* I'd whisper as I read. Could there be a dream just temporarily deferred wallowing in those drooping denims and triple-x sweats, could there be a poet wrapped tight against the world in those swaddling clothes?

He was the writer then, but now, reluctant resident of the Middlesex County House of Correction, he is *the* writer, sanctioned by the baddest of badasses because he has trumpeted the power of twisting verb and noun not only to say things, but to *get* shit:

They paying me to write love letters to their ladies.
I write poems if they rather have that,
this one big musclehead brother everybody be sweatin
even asked me to write a letter to his mama on her birthday.

They call him Scribe.

They bring him their imploded dreams, letters from their women-in-waiting tired of waiting. On deadline, he spins impossible sugar onto the precise lines of legal pads, pens June/moon dripping enough to melt a b-girl's hard heart. He drops to scarred knees, moans and whimpers in stilted verse, coaxing last ink from a passed-around ballpoint, making it wail:

please please babygirl,
don't be talking about not waiting out my time,
only five years left, that ain't much,
hey Scribe, Scribe, hook me up, man,
I ain't got no answer for this shit she sudden talkin.

Tattooed in riotous colors, they circle him in the common room, whispering to him beneath the surface of their reputations:

Got a job for you Scribe, got a job.

When the letters are crafted just right, copied over and over and edited for the real, the customers stumble through the aloud reading of them, scared of their own new voices. Too dazzled to demand definition, they scrunch scarred foreheads and whistle through gold caps at the three-syllable kickverbs:

I'm gon' trust you, they tell my son. *I'm gon' trust you on this.*
They don't want their softness. They don't want it.

You know, Scribe, damn, damn this shit SINGS!
You blessed man, you blessed.
I don't know what you saying man, but it sho sound good.
So I'm gon' trust you. I'm gon' trust you on this.

Then they copy the words in their own hand and send spun silk shoutouts to the freewalking world, hoping that a disillusioned girlfriend or a neglected mother or a wife-in-waiting tired of waiting will slit open the envelope and feel a warm repentant soul spill out into her hands.

And I must admit, as a fellow poet, I envy my son, this being necessary. Think of it. Which of us would refuse to try on the first face of a killer, our life teetering on every line? Wouldn't we want to craft a new front for everyone just once, to rewrite one moment of a life story, to beg for mercy on behalf of someone who has never known life on his knees?

And at the end of our flowery betrayal, that white-heat moment of no sound. In the steamy pocket of it, all we'd need is one person rising up slow, full of spit and menace, to say:

O.K., O.K., I'm gon' trust you on that one.
I'm gon' have to trust you on that.

THE CIRCUS IS IN TOWN

And this time there's trouble.
Whistle-toothed carnies
blow their wretched sugar
into strained balloons of blood.
God's beasts, inflamed and loony
in unlatched cages, fuck furiously
across all species—lion with grizzly,
ape with his keeper.

The alligator woman claws at a hell
of skin, listens to her cunt snap shut,
and shrieks at what the moon has told her.
The baby floating in a jar lists to the left,
bumps its head hard against the glass,
slowly reveals a worming eye. The vague
chaos brings a smile to his swirling.

And I am standing on an old roller coaster
whipping through the dark. A sculpted lion's
head leers from the first car, one marbled eye
lost long ago to wind. No ropes, belts, or bars
bind my body. There is nothing to keep me
from flying loose and slamming against that
building with its ghostly cadre of bumper cars.
The ragged clack of my rises and dips disturb
and intrigue the growl-faced boy and the woman
balancing her sex on three misshapen legs.

Their milky, eager eyes flap locked,
turn up, upward.

I do not fall,
and this amazes me, amazes them.
Yet still I go faster,
the speed biting holes in my hair,
whittling scream to whisper,
blurring tempera clown leers.
The damned thing squeals up, up,
hugging the rickety matchstick track,
ribboning the sheet of grease-scented dark.
Up this insanely, the air boasts a simple pain,
and I gulp breath as feverishly
as the alligator girl scratches her skin
to find a soft, definite history beneath.

Watch me.
Watch along with the limber,
the slithering,
the toothless,
the doomed.
Dance in gleeful anticipation
of my plummet to the midway.
Stand by until I have fallen.
Let the freaks sniff out the parts they need.
Then separate the splinters of wood
from those of bone.

HER OTHER NAME

for Girl X, Chicago

The first thing we took away was your name.
We erased the bleak shame from each syllable,
blurred the image of your tiny body broken into
network sound bytes, snippets of videotape
with a swollen face x-ed out.
x   as in she is no longer a good girl.
x   as in two simple lines crossing
where a beating heart should be.

You were little, like we don't want to remember.
You were stutter-folded, you were beaten liquid
on those lonely stairs, your skin was slashed,
you were raped with a fist and sticks, insecticide
sprayed into your seeing and down the tunnel of
your throat. He must have held your mouth open,
stretching the circle, leaving moons in your lip.
The violation left you blind and without tongue,
wrecked the new clock of you. You were jump rope
in double time and pigeon-toed, navy blue Keds
with round toes and soles like paper, jelly sandwiches
and grape smash fingers, you, ashy-kneed rose,
missing rib, splintered and flinching through
a death sleep. In which direction do we pray?

To recreate you, they relied on ritual.
Weeping nurses gently parted your hair, the teeth

of the comb tipped in rubber, and dried blood
showered from your scalp like chips of paint.
They rubbed warm oil through the unraveling braids,
threaded ribbon through to the ends.
We will give you back your life
by pretending you are still alive.
Lowering your x into a tub of warm water, they
scrubbed you with stinging soap, sang songs filled
with light and lyric, then dabbed you dry with those
brutal sickbed towels, avoiding the left nipple,
smashed before it began. Wrapping you in the stiff garb
of virgins, they told you that you were healed,
there in that stark room of beeping machines
and blood vials and sterilized silver, they built you
a child's body and coaxed your battered heart back inside.

Girl
x. The violation left. x
you blind and x voiceless

And they braided your hair every day, gently,
the ritual insane, strands over, under, through, over,
under, through, fingers locked in languid weave,
until the same of it all brought your voice back.

The nurses cheered, told you they'd found a cure
for history, that the unreal would refuse to be real.
Soon you'll be able to see again, they whispered.
I know you never meant to be ungrateful, my rib,
when you rose up half and growled this grace:

that's
that's
O.K. you
can keep
my
eyes

FORGOTTEN IN ALL THIS

In the scarred fresco Joseph
is the outline, eluding.
Under close eye, the rotted color
may reveal a beard,
a muted and battered halo,
one sullen eye cast toward
the wrapped and luminous swaddle
that became the world,
damning what the world was before.
His wife, earth hips in flawed marble
or thick tempera, is spoiled and yes,
blessed silly, already beyond him,
not needing to acknowledge a mere man
etched as afterthought among sheep.

What's left of his head is always in his hands.

Crinkled and cracking backdrop
of *Sacra Familia,* he is tagged dispensable
whenever the three are considered.
The child and mother are polished,
redeemed, lifted almost to breathing.
Their color deafens. He is crutch,
inn searcher, tonal balance, ampersand,
weary of squinting against the rays of the son.

Artist, look again at him.
Give him back his eyes,
the burnished cheek.
Draw him whirling, furious about all this.
Make him holy beyond canvas,
chisel, and the saying so.
Brushstroke him a mouth that moves,
with teeth that clench and assert.
Let his wails wash over us,
we who rendered him no brighter than hill and oxen,
we who always knew his name but never who he was.

DOWN 4 THE UP STROKE

for Danny Solis

But you have poetry, you say.
And if you can tell me what poetry is,
where the line is drawn
between the beauty and the breathing
of breath into something to make it beautiful,
I will claim poetry as my own.

Poets, when last breath sought to seduce,
your mojo flashed skinned nerve to the open air.
You bitched and cajoled until I was pissed enough
to assign you the task of my wounds.
You said *Patricia,*
come to us if the world bleeds through.
You drove in from the city and backhanded me
with your clunky rhymes, your limp couplets,
your falterings, your leaps for the sky,
your lean and joyless works in progress.
You jumped up and down on my heart,
yelling *beat beat,*
when I was June's only sin, you screeched
beat beat,
when there was nothing I could do but be a liar
flat under everyone, you angled storm boot heels
at my chest until the irritation warmed dead muscle
and pulled it onto the dance floor. Ignore the mic static.
What unflinching poems spring from the mouths
of the almost dead. I could never love me like this.

WOMEN ARE TAUGHT

I'm convinced it's a man's smell that pulls us in—
faux leather and spiced soap, splashes of lemon
and Old Spice, the odd oil tinging his sweat.
As women, we were designed to wither beneath
the mingled stench of them. As a woman, I was

yo, yo, baby work that big ass, you must want
designed
what I got
to wither
c'mon honey just let daddy stick it in a little bit
beneath
bitch of course i love you i give you money don't i

Why else would i cage myself in glorious raiment
of spandex and lace, paint my panting the hues
of burn, twist my voice from madam to smoke?
Why else, once he has left me, do I bury my face
in the place his sex has pressed, inhale
what he has left, and pray to die there?

On the day I married, I was such porcelain,
delicate and poised to shatter. I was unflinching,
sure of my practiced vows,
already addicted to the sanctity of bondage.
I was an unfurled ballad in a scoop-necked
sheath carved of sugar. And him on my arm,

grinning like a bear, all sinew and swagger.
Bibles were everywhere. Dizzied by rote,
I stared at the gold rope around my finger.
He owned me.
And that felt nice.
That felt right.

the first time i hit her
I thought the loose tooth a temporary nightmare
the second time i hit her
He cried himself to sleep, and that was nice,
that was right
the third time i hit her
He counted my scars and whispered *never again*
baby never again

When *i'd die without you*
turned to *i'll kill you if you ever leave me*
I bristled like a hound in heat, I didn't
understand the not being aroused, when
let's get away
turned to
you'll never get away
such heat rippled my
belly such crave in me screeching *walk run run run*

run
i etched a thin line into the throat of her running
run
i stalked streets just a breath behind her
run

i shattered our son's skull with a shotgun
run
i wanted her dead.

My first thought as he jammed the
still smoking barrel into my breastbone
her first thought
as the blade mapped my chest, the
hammer sliced the air toward my hair
the bullet pushed me through a plate glass window
my last thought *you won't believe this*
my last thought
you really won't believe this
my last thought
was
he must really

love me

LOOK AT 'EM GO

for my granddaughter Mikaila

Hard-sewn, soft-belly, huff, hip swing,
teeny woman catapult, dings in the walls
of your body. I know your scars, badges
earned in the grave pursuit of science—
jump rope whips along a curve of calf,
toes stubbed purple, tender uncolored
patches of skin woven shut over your
small traumas. Wily dervish, you flip,
hurtle, fly, daily rattle your soft spine,
send your bones to the wailing places.
This is play in the age of *Grandma, who
knocked those buildings down?* This is
8 years old in the age of could-die-soon.
This is life as collision and scrape, hard
lessons in the poetics of risk. Daring
the world to harm us, you pull hard
on my hand. *Grandma, let's run!* We laugh
and trip as the sidewalk sniffs our skin
and stars along our path flame shut.
Die fast, die slow, die giggling, die anyway.
Our speed tempts the Reaper as I shelter
you in this first death, the loss of our throats.

STOP THE PRESSES

My job is to draw the pictures no one can voice,
to soothe and bellow toward the numbed heart,
to breathe in your chronicles, discuss them out
in lines weak enough for you to read and swallow.
My mouth is a jumble of canine teeth, I bite only
at the official whistle. My job is sexy leads for the
bones clattering in your closet, to sing you sated
each night with a forgettable soundtrack of paper
and ink. I am neat, easily folded, a sifter of truth
born to be burned. I count your dead, fathom their
stories, bless them with long, flexible histories
and their final names. There are no soft stanzas
in this city of curb sleep and murdered children.
We need soft words for hard things, this silk
brushing the inevitability of rock. Birth truth in
this way, just once. Craft the news and overcome
all that you ever were—a reason to turn the page.

WHAT YOU PRAY TOWARD

"The orgasm has replaced the cross as the focus of longing and the image of fulfillment."
   —Malcolm Muggeridge, 1966

I.

Hubbie 1 used to get wholly pissed when I made
myself come. *I'm right here!,* he'd sputter, blood
popping to the surface of his fuzzed cheeks,
goddamn it, I'm right here! By that time, I was
in no mood to discuss the myriad merits of my
pointer, or to jam the brakes on the express train
slicing through my blood. It was easier to suffer
the practiced professorial huff, the hissed invectives
and the cold old shoulder, liver-dotted, quaking
with rage. Shall we pause to bless professors and
codgers and their bellowed, unquestioned ownership
of things? I was sneaking time with my own body.
I know I signed something over, but it wasn't that.

II.

No matter how I angle this history, it's weird,
so let's just say *Bringing Up Baby* was on the telly
and suddenly my lips pressing against
the couch cushions felt spectacular and I thought
wow this is strange, what the hell, I'm 30 years old,
am I dying down there is this the feel, does the cunt
go to heaven first, ooh, snapped river, ooh shimmy
I had never had it never knew, oh I clamored and
lurched beneath my little succession of boys I cried
writhed hissed, ooh wee, suffered their flat lapping

and machine-gun diddling their insistent c'mon girl
c'mon until I memorized the blueprint for drawing
blood from their shoulders, until there was nothing
left but the self-satisfied liquidy snore of he who has
rocked she, he who has made she weep with script.
But this, oh Cary, gee Katherine, hallelujah Baby,
the fur do fly, all gush and kaboom on the wind.

III.

Don't hate me because I am multiple, hurtling.
As long as there is still skin on the pad of my finger,
as long as I'm awake, as long as my (new) husband's
mouth holds out, I am the spinner, the unbridled,
the bellowing freak. When I have emptied him,
he leans back, coos, edges me along, keeps wondering
count. He falls to his knees in front of it, marvels
at my yelps and carousing spine, stares unflinching
as I bleed spittle onto the pillows.
He has married a witness.
My body bucks, slave to its selfish engine,
and love is the dim miracle of these little deaths,
fracturing, speeding for the surface.

IV.

We know the record. As it taunts us, we have giggled,
considered stopwatches, little laboratories. Somewhere
beneath the suffering clean, swathed in eyes and silver,
she came 134 times in one hour. I imagine wires holding
her tight, her throat a rattling window. Searching scrubbed
places for her name, I find only reams of numbers. I ask
the quietest of them:

V.

Are we God?

WHAT MEN DO WITH THEIR MOUTHS

for cr avery

cue the frenzied combo of molar and spit, his tongue
touches every chroma on its way to blue. he deftly
conjures washboards and rubber, even suburban
girls lie still for the twinging, the humid reckoning.

i want to coax last night's corona from his chin, rub
my index finger along the surface of his laugh, pull
it open to check the throat's slick road. something
illegal's going on down there, the sweet keening
of ancient instruments. wonder boy opens beauteous
and words become both otherwise and everything.

DREAM DEAD DADDY WALKING

You don't have to be asleep to dream. At any time,
cue the untruths. You can believe, for instance,
that your dead father isn't dead anymore.
There is the doorbell clanging and your one-year-old
screeching *Granddaddy!,* lurching and running
to the banister to risk his life looking over,
and yes, there is a curving staircase, partially awash
in sun, and your father skipping stairs,
grinning gold tooth, growling *Hey Meathead*
to his yelping grandson. Your unslept story freezes
right here, with his bony brown face upturned,
you and your leaping baby looking down at him.
The clock locks on this.
The raucous welcome stops, he does not take
another step, nothing moves but his face,
slipping out of sun into dead again. I am alone
in my office, terrified of conjuring him,
but there is the clanging, the boy screeching,
the gold tooth, those slats of June, the son,
the father, the daughter seeing all of what has
already happened happening,
and the soft remembered thud of wingtips.

WRITING EXERCISE BREATHING OUTSIDE MY BINDER

I'm as trapped as a housefly
in a vagrant's unwashed beard.
Yesterday's stinging snapshots:
fatty salted meat grilling madly,
a dying bulb sputtering heat and speckles of light,
Mama's keloid-scarred cheek suffering pink foundation.
To balance that then with this now,
I gulp potent cocktails
of fluoxetine and chardonnay, and confess
that I am partial to crying jags
and this thing James Taylor coos:
Here comes another gray morning,
a not so good morning after all. . . .

I itch that scratch
before the refrain of the real
fades and forces me back
to my $50-a-week white woman.
Our current topic:
I collapse beneath touches.
What rises me is the relentless
march of seconds, guffawing weirdly,
all dressed in their heaven-bound church hats
and ripped little gowns.

THE THRILL IS ON

Inspired by the B.B. King/Eric Clapton video "Riding with the King"

Side touching side, they lean one into the other,
hugging guitars tighter than a wise man holds
onto a wandering gal, which is tight as he can clutch
without actually chaining her to the slippery surface
of his heart. The Lord promised to age B.B. the way all
bluesmen age, decorating him with a sweet snag
in his hip, a solo lecherous eye, and an abundance
of tales peppered and fueled by 'ssissippi sun and just
one more fried something—*I know, I know, it ain't no*
good for me, but hell, I'm from down South, and down
there grease is a damn food group. For so long, he was
grand marshal for the calling of the catfish. Now history
threatens to overwhelm, pulling him to earth with pills
and needles, diluting the crimson kick in his blood.
I didn't want to see the hasty Afro grow silvery sparse,
didn't need his sugar sickness unwrapped on prime time,
certainly didn't ever want to hear the blue grunt falter
as if, rehashing his woe, he had inhaled a pocket of air.

Once, in a cluttered Newport trailer, B.B. leaned forward,
touched a hammy hand to my forehead, insisted I was
hiding a piece of some angel. The voltage left his chapped
palm, sliced through like hooch, and settled restlessly
in the south of me. They cast the most remarkable spells,
these blue fathers. See how the guitar connects directly
to the belly. They dazzle with sharkskin and gold incisor,

work roots and moaning conjures, teach Northern children
the waning language of screen doors and spent matches.

Rotund on 2/4 time, impossibly sexy with all that misery
in him, B.B. laughs with his mouth wide open, serves up
a glimpse of old glitter, the odd pork sliver. The two of them
climb growl-first into that Caddy to cruise streets saddled
with old Negro names, streets where loose women beckon,
brothers check out the rims and storefronts spit glass teeth.
B.B. fills that backseat again and again in a circular tuxedo,
pearl buttons popping, bow tie lost forever under all that neck.
Craving my blue daddy, I scramble into that car, grab hold.
Clapton, looking like everybody's picture of Jesus, floors it,
hurtling three old fools toward a common key, an enviable end.

BLUES THROUGH 2 BONE

Her daddy was ashed grooved hands,
tree trunk man, rock in the A.M.E.
and haul a righteous hymn all the way
up from his skinned toes home.
His shrine at the kitchen table,
dousing Mama's overwhupped
starches with Tabasco fire,
gotta make it worth the biting,
peppered heat stinkin' an inch
from all of his skin. Baby girl
he'd whisper, baby girl baby girl
baby girl, splintered palm pressed
into her belly, kicking hard denims
away from his ankles, losing
his thumbs in her hair, clawing loose
Sunday plaits, saying with muscle clench
and crunchy candy that she was
wide shoulder pretty, sweet leg
double dutch jumping pretty,
more color than was ever even necessary.
Underneath a pissed blanket, she waited
for teacher. She loved the rough universe
of his left hand, and how he said she was so black
he needed directions to get to her

in the dark.

FIREMAN

Some days he'd slowly spin his dizzying
street corner arc, a circle he swore
was defined by angels. *And they is black
ones, too!* he'd declare, never daring
beyond heavenly prescribed boundary.
Fireman wrecked Otis Redding lyric,
spewed misaligned gospel, regaled us
with his tales of recent visits to a hell
that was preparing to receive us all.
Sizzling Chi days, he'd whirl furious,
shower the one or two feet beyond
himself with stinging spittle, preach
and pontificate through the blur. After
sudden stops, he'd lean against the bus
shelter to undizzy. *Lawd ham mercy,* he'd
moan, while the world turned upside
in and Mama and I cut a road around him.
Long time before, Fireman had raced
face-first into a blaze trying to save
something belonged to him, a dog
or a woman or some other piece of life,
and an explosion had blown his face
straight back, you know, sometimes
I hate words, they don't know how
to say anything, imagine that I am digging
my fingers deep into the clay of my face
and pulling, watch how my eyes get,

how they can't stop seeing the last thing
they saw, his eyelashes gone, eyebrows
gone, everything on his head headed
backwards, like it was trying to get
away from him. Maps all over his skin,
maps for little lost people, everybody
this way, back, his nose smashed flat
and headed back, back, smoke-dimmed
teeth tiny tiles in his mouth, can't pull
bulbous pink lips together because
of skin fused to skin, no end to that stiff
horrible smile. In my dream, I rest the full
of my hand against his fuming torso,
daring it a place there, chanting ice.
Not knowing this sudden love, Fireman bolts
and resumes his dance, whirling, waiting,
charred limbs outstretched. From his
monstrous mouth, wrong Otis strains
to be louder than that November day,
that bone heat, those shattering windows.

PSYCHE!

*"Piscataway, NJ (AP)—Researchers at Rutgers University have developed
a trio of drugs they believe can destroy HIV."*
—*Dec.* 12 in New York Newsday, *the* Toronto Globe and Mail
and hundreds of newspapers around the world

"Rutgers researchers say new drug stops HIV in its tracks."
—Washington Blade, *Dec.* 17

"New class of AIDS drugs 'could be it.'"
—New Orleans Times-Picayune, *Dec.* 18

*"Press stories in mid Dec. 2004 about an AIDS breakthrough from Rutgers
University and elsewhere were exaggerated in the media."*
—AIDS Treatment News

many more than that many,
this hallelujah, this bruise Jesus
all over purpled ankle, more than
this scrubbed silver and next needle
this whole heart in an african hand
much more than these drum digits
this possible this wait a minute what
does this say this page 47, more than
this mad, this unlatched, this bandage
and gut swirling, what stiff number
was the blanket, scissored felt
and eye buttons, glitter elmer glued
to gone outlines, names too simple
to be so hard pronounced. more

than that, even more than conjured
million, this cock/tail, this twitch
and drool, this vomit, this legislation.

RELATED TO THE BUTTERCUP,
BLOOMS IN SPRING

I.

What do we do with these huge gifts of the throat and tongue?
How do we manage?

II.

I used to believe that nobody but me could see
the stars shimmering riot outside my window.
Mama, my stars are here, I'd say, *my stars.*
I welcomed them with a notebook, toothmarked Bic,
and teeny revolutions crammed into the stingy space
of a college-ruled line. I wrote until the precise script
wandered, until the stars blinked themselves dim
and said *good-night Patricia Ann, it's late even for us*
and it hurts to watch how hard you dream.

One morning, I woke to find whole pages filled
with a single word—*anemone.* Over and over, ens
and ems straining to stern Palmer Method hilltops.
Anemone. Anemone.

Ms. Stein,
I can't explain the dizzy I felt the day you chalked
that word on the board and said,
Who can pronounce this?
I wish I could grant you breath here,
but all I recall is dark hair vaguely flipped, a slight sour

to you, and the wary smile of a young Jewish girl
teaching on Walnut Street, just down the block
from your million miles away.
Funny, how you twisted me
by introducing a word
you figured would stump us all,
funny how I bellowed the odd accents
and a light grew slow and unbeckoned behind your eyes.

That one word was sweet silver on my new tongue,
it kept coming back to my mouth,
it was the very first sound I wanted to own,
to name myself after,
I wanted no one else to ever utter this.
Even now, listen to how *anemone*
circles, turns round, and surprises itself.
That day I gave that word a home just under my breath
and at least a hundred times
I drew on the drug of it, serving it up to the needing air.
All this before I knew what it meant.

(If you never remember feeling that way about a single word,
sensing a burn in the sheer power of its sound, lift up
your poetry—all those thick, important pages—and see that
it is resting on nothing. Then shred those sheets, toss them
to sky, and lie prone beneath the empty flutter. You must
own one word completely before you can claim another.)

Ms. Stein, go ahead,
make me nine again, take me back
to when I wasn't afraid of anything

except long division and the words *Go pull me off a switch,*
when Karen Ford and I pulled our panties down
and wriggled up against each other for new taboo,

Ms. Stein, I couldn't *stop* writing.
I wrote myself angled and tress-topped,
I wrote myself hero, I wrote myself white,
Cherokee, cheerleader, distressed damsel in Alan Ladd's arms,
I wrote myself winged, worshipped, I wrote long stories
where I was always the primary twinkle, the beacon,
inevitably envied. I wrote *anemone* over and over
in rigid hand, the loops and hilltops perfect.

Anemone. Anemone.

When I was nine, the barbershops left their doors open
and all manner of glorious bullshit spilled out,
charms and curses spritzed with that mango oil
that makes black heads shimmer. Balls of sliced nap
slip sliding the tile, my people razzing and razored,
the dozens in effect, sentence songs, spontaneous doo-wop
where any two lines came together to make a corner.
I was little woman, sweet little crumbsnatcher,
baby you a pretty one,
won't be long before those boys start sniffing around.
I'd squeeze my eyes shut, loving those hold-on lies.

I knew these men would have a place in my stories,
crowns wobbling on sculpted scalp, all their
ain't done beens and *musta haves* and *done gone for goods*
languaging the air of the world I had waiting.

I wrote their bodies arcing over mine,
their Lucky Struck smooches on the top of my head,
their lifting me and whirling me 'round
till nothing made sense but the spin. I wrote about
that damned heartbreak in their eyes, miles north
of the heart, how they stayed mad all morning
at that whiskey bottle. I heard them talk about women
with both craving and knives in their throats. Together,
we waited for the stars.
Come on in here baby, they'd say, *always carrying that notebook.*
Come on in here and sit in this chair and write me something pretty.

Ms. Stein, you unlatched this fever. Wherever you are,
may you be blessed by whatever God means to you.

Anemone.
A sweet beginning I can hide in my mouth.
I live on its taste when my pen won't move.

WHEN DEXTER KING MET JAMES EARL RAY

There was a tender in them both, a place picked raw.
As Southern men do, shirts buttoned hard across the throat,
the clasping of hands that know weather,
eye linked to eye, unflinching, the flat-toned, muttered *how-do*.
How do you?
And the scripted respect, the pudge-cheeked preacher
inquiring idly after the dying man's days.
Whole wars in them, but just a single rupture.
Their halos florid, overglowing, some news reporter
hissing expectantly into a dead silver mic: *Say it, say it.*
James Earl liver-toned, wobbling on old bone,
one lazy eye perked for it.
It.
The King rolls his R's, throats elegant, sweats bullets
into his collar. Having shaved too keenly, his beard
is peppered red, whispering blood. And still the pleasantries.
Exactly how does one go from commenting on the weather
It's hot. Awful humid. Smells like more rain to asking *did*
you frame my father's head in your gun sight,
did you empty his dinner chair,
lonely my nights,
pull back on that trigger?

Go on, get it out, boy. I'm dying heah.
Cameras whir.

The men are like fools, silent, damned respectful,
exactly a yardstick between them. And it's the windup, the pitch:
Sir, I have to ask you, sir, my kind sir, excuse me,
I hate to bother you sir, but I have to ask for the record,
Did you kill my father?
And if the answer is yes, will there be a throttling, an errant
sob, a small silver pistol slipped from an inside pocket?
And if the answer is no, will there be a throttling, an errant
sob, a small silver pistol slipped from an inside pocket?
Time has a way of growing things all huge,
lifting up our lives to shove in the splinter.
But, surprisingly, James Earl resists double take, and the wide-eye.
No, I didn't. No, sir. No.

That settles it then, that settles it.
And we're locked on this limp drama long after the credits roll
and *Hollywood Squares* has taken over,
long after the network has anthemed and dimmed to snow.
Time for some corn chips and a brew.
Time to fall asleep with a clear head.
Time to celebrate the slow sweet of Southern men.
It's time to rejoice in the fact that nobody killed nobody,
and high time to forget that somebody died anyway.

ALL HIS DISTRESSING DISGUISES

"Every day, I see Jesus Christ in all His distressing disguises."
—Mother Teresa

Which explains why I am tempted to kiss the hand
of the flushed minion shoving me aside for a perch
on the # 4. There is much immediate in him,
so much otherwise and elsewhere, I presume
he is famous in some spectacular way, who can say?
I believe that holy rests in the simple.

So I scan the skin of the *Post* vendor looking
for flecks of gold, I plot to touch the singed fingers
of the fry cook as he passes me eggs done wrong.
I listen for wisdom in the flailing screech of the B-boy
whose earbuds transport him to a place where
swagger is sanctified. Noting my brash appraisal,
he thrusts his little sex forward, which could indeed
be a blessing of sorts. The idea I pray toward could
be the drama critic with a pinky toe fetish
or the bottle of whiskey left burning at his bedside.

Or maybe my God is the man who heat-seeks
my areolas, forgets my birth, leaves clumps of Kung Pao
in the sink to tempt Westchester's reticent roaches.

He is so simply holy, spent, and slightly crazed
after climax. Damn, he *does* glow. How ironic
if my savior were a mere Bruce, his New England
stammer blessing my quest, kinking the gifted halo.

TEAHOUSE OF THE ALMIGHTY
July 17, 2002, Brockton, MA

Peppermint bites at the back of the teeth,
heat prickles points on an unready tongue.
The solemn eyes of Jesus contemplate from
black light: *My child, you will conquer the spice.*
You will swallow. Every blend, from rose hip
to green, is sharp saccharine and colored
like blood. The menu, scrawled in Sharpie
on gray shirt cardboard, is blotched with
smoke, and, anyway, nothing has a price.

Splintered wood seats, carved across with
curses and desperate two-syllabled prayers,
strain to hold the quivering weight of
the devoted and the hard questions poised
by their thirst. Wherever it is not stained
or peeled back or missing, the tile floor
is scarred with sloping Scripture written
from the position of the knees—*As far as*
the east is from the west, so far hath he
removed our transgressions from us.
Men with rheumy gazes arc over teacups,
sip cleansing and penance. Their suit coats,
once special at Sears, are ironed hard,
growing too airy, are inevitably brown.

The waitress, Glorie, a spit-curled kingdom,
is spritzed, flip-tongued, ripped too suddenly

from a Southern soil. She say: *'Fore you ask,*
what we got here is Domino sugar, thick cream.
From a seat near the reeking john, a crinkled
alto quavers, a choir by its ownself: *I love*
the Lord, he heard my cry. Miss Glorie stops,
shows the palm of her hand to heaven.
All faith, it is believed, lies in testimony.

The voice is old church, teetering, dim-visioned,
pink foam rollers in thin, hard-oiled strands.
It is northbound Greyhound, shucked beans,
buttercake, chicken necks in waxed paper,
trapped against their own oil. The voice belongs
to the m'dear of red dust, to our daily dying mothers,
to every single city's west side. It wears aged lace
and A-lines hemmed with masking tape.
The woman wails sanctified because the heat
has singed her fingers, because a huge empty
sits across from her and breathes a little death
onto the folds of her face. *I'll take another cup,*
she says. *I believe I will. But don't be scared,*
Glorie, make it hot. Put some fire under it.
Lord can't tell I'm here 'less I holla out loud.

She rocks the day dim, sips slow, props the comma
of her spine against the hard wood. But she snaps
straight whenever the door opens.
He's gon' come.
He knows the place.
A man gets thirsty.

RUNNING FOR ARETHA

for Louis Brown, Boston

I blew out my speakers today listening to Aretha
sing gospel. "Take My Hand, Precious Lord"
crackled and popped until finally the tweeters
smoked and the room grew silent, although,
as my mama would say, *The spirit kept kickin'*.
Humming fitfully between sips of spiced tea,
I decided that salvation didn't need a soundtrack.

Boston is holding its breath, flirting with snow.
Upstairs, plugged into M.C. somebody, my son
is oblivious to headlines. The world is a gift,
just waiting for his fingers to loose the ribbon.

He won't find out until later that a boy with his
face, his swagger, his common veil, died crumpled
on a Dorchester street. He will turn away from
tonight's filmed probings into the boy's short stay,
stutterings from stunned grandmammas,
neighbors slowly shaking their heads. He'll pretend
not to see the clip of the paramedics screaming
obscenities at the boy's heart, turning its stubborn
key with their fists. *Want anything, Ma?* he'll ask
from the kitchen, where he has skulked for shelter,
for a meal of sugar and bread to block his throat.

The crisp, metallic stench of the busted speakers
reminds me that there are other things to do.
My computer hums seductively.
My husband hints that he may want to argue about sex.
I think about starting a fire, but don't think I can stand
the way the paper curls, snaps, and dissolves into ash.
So I climb the stairs to my son's room,
rest my head against the door's cold wood,
listen to the muffled roars of rappers. But I don't knock.
He deserves one more moment of not knowing that boy's face,
how I ran to Aretha's side, how tight the ribbon is tied.

WHEN THE BURNING BEGINS

for Otis Douglas Smith, my father

The recipe for hot water cornbread is simple:
Cornmeal, hot water. Mix till sluggish,
then dollop in a sizzling skillet.
When you smell the burning begin, flip it.
When you smell the burning begin again,
dump it onto a plate. You've got to wait
for the burning and get it just right.

Before the bread cools down,
smear it with sweet salted butter
and smash it with your fingers,
crumple it up in a bowl
of collard greens or buttermilk,
forget that I'm telling you it's the first thing
I ever cooked, that my daddy was laughing
and breathing and no bullet in his head
when he taught me.

Mix it till it looks like quicksand, he'd say.
Till it moves like a slow song sounds.

We'd sit there in the kitchen, licking our fingers
and laughing at my mother,
who was probably scrubbing something with bleach,
or watching *Bonanza,*
or thinking how stupid it was to be burning

that nasty old bread in that cast iron skillet.
When I told her that I'd made my first-ever pan
of hot water cornbread, and that my daddy
had branded it glorious, she sniffed and kept
mopping the floor over and over in the same place.

So here's how you do it:

You take out a bowl, like the one
we had with blue flowers and only one crack,
you put the cornmeal in it.
Then you turn on the hot water and you let it run
while you tell the story about the boy
who kissed your cheek after school
or about how you really want to be a reporter
instead of a teacher or nurse like Mama said,
and the water keeps running while Daddy says
You will be a wonderful writer
and you will be famous someday and when
you get famous, if I wrote you a letter and
sent you some money, would you write about me?

and he is laughing and breathing and no bullet
in his head. So you let the water run into this mix
till it moves like mud moves at the bottom of a river,
which is another thing Daddy said, and even though
I'd never even seen a river,
I knew exactly what he meant.
Then you turn the fire way up under the skillet,
and you pour in this mix
that moves like mud moves at the bottom of a river,
like quicksand, like slow song sounds.

That stuff pops something awful when it first hits
that blazing skillet, and sometimes Daddy and I
would dance to those angry pop sounds,
he'd let me rest my feet on top of his
while we waltzed around the kitchen
and my mother huffed and puffed
on the other side of the door. *When you are famous,*
Daddy asks me, *will you write about dancing*
in the kitchen with your father?
I say everything I write will be about you,
then you will be famous too. And we dip and swirl
and spin, but then he stops.
And sniffs the air.

The thing you have to remember
about hot water cornbread
is to wait for the burning
so you know when to flip it, and then again
so you know when it's crusty and done.
Then eat it the way we did,
with our fingers,
our feet still tingling from dancing.
But remember that sometimes the burning
takes such a long time,
and in that time,
sometimes,

poems are born.

COLOPHON

Teahouse of the Almighty was designed at Coffee House Press, in the historic
warehouse district of downtown Minneapolis. Fonts include Perpetua and Scala Sans.

FUNDER ACKNOWLEDGMENTS

Coffee House Press is an independent nonprofit literary publisher. Our books are made
possible through the generous support of grants and gifts from many foundations, cor-
porate giving programs, individuals, and through state and federal support. This book
received special project support from the National Poetry Series and the Witter Bynner
Foundation. Coffee House Press receives general operating support from the Minnesota
State Arts Board, through an appropriation by the Minnesota State Legislature and from
the National Endowment for the Arts. Coffee House receives major funding from the
McKnight Foundation, and from Target. Coffee House also receives significant support
from: an anonymous donor; the Elmer and Eleanor Andersen Foundation; the Buuck
Family Foundation; the Bush Foundation; the Patrick and Aimee Butler Family
Foundation; the Foundation for Contemporary Arts; Stephen and Isabel Keating; the
Outagamie Foundation; the Pacific Foundation; the law firm of Schwegman, Lundberg,
Woessner & Kluth, P.A.; the James R. Thorpe Foundation; the Archie D. and Bertha H.
Walker Foundation; TLR/West; the Woessner Freeman Family Foundation; and many
other generous individual donors.

*This activity is made possible
in part by a grant from the
Minnesota State Arts Board,
through an appropriation by the
Minnesota State Legislature
and a grant from the National
Endowment for the Arts.* MINNESOTA
STATE ARTS BOARD

NATIONAL
ENDOWMENT
FOR THE ARTS

TARGET.

To you and our many readers across the country,
we send our thanks for your continuing support.

Good books are brewing at coffeehousepress.org